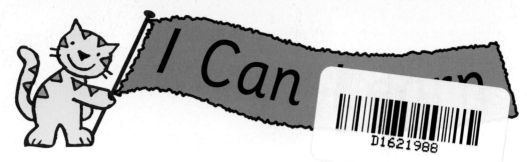

I Can Read Words

lion

Written by Nicola Morgan

Illustrated by John Haslam

This book belongs to

MYKA JAI

EGMONT

Tips for happy home learning

Make learning fun by working at your child's pace
and always giving tasks which s/he can do.
Tasks that are too difficult will discourage her/him
from trying again.

Give encouragement and praise and remember
to award gold stars and sticker badges for
effort as well as good work.

Always do too little rather than too much,
and finish each session on a positive note.

Don't work when you or your child
is tired or hungry.

Reinforce workbook activities and new ideas by
making use of real objects around the home.

EGMONT
We bring stories to life

Published in Great Britain by Egmont Books Limited,
239 Kensington High Street, London W8 6SA
www.egmont.co.uk

Printed in Italy.
ISBN 1 4052 1550 X
2 4 6 8 10 9 7 5 3

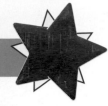

Hello! I'm Curly Cat.

I'm going to teach you to read. Look closely at these letters and join the ones which are the same.

a   o   g

e   c   d

s   c   e

a   g   d

s   o

Well done! That was clever.

These are more tricky.
You need to look very very carefully.

This page is for lots of practice. On each line, circle the one that matches the one on the left.

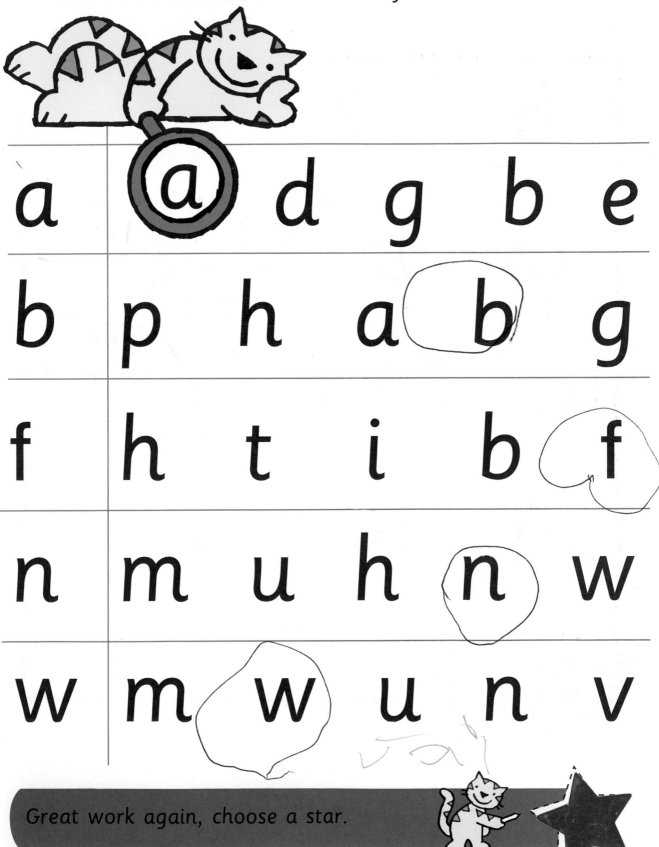

a	@	d	g	b	e
b	p	h	a	(b)	g
f	h	t	i	b	(f)
n	m	u	h	(n)	w
w	m	(w)	u	n	v

We can put letters together to make real words. Ask a grown-up to write your name here. Use lower case, except for the first letter.

 MYKA Jai

Here are all the letters. Put a circle round all the ones you see in your name.

 a b c d e f g h i j k l m n

o p q r s t u v w x y z

Ask a grown-up to help you write the names of two friends here:

BRIA

Look back at the letters in the alphabet.
Put a **red** circle round those you need for the **first** name and a **blue** circle round those you need for the **second** name.

Let's look at words now.
Join the same words with a line.

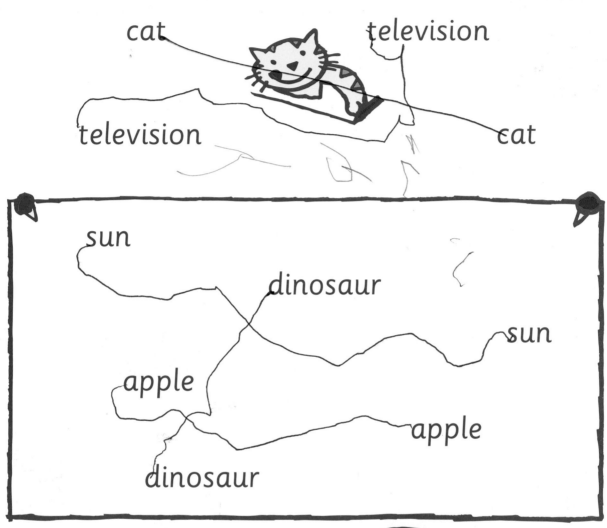

cat   television

television   cat

sun

dinosaur

sun

apple

apple

dinosaur

Do the same with the
words above.

Here are some more words to match.

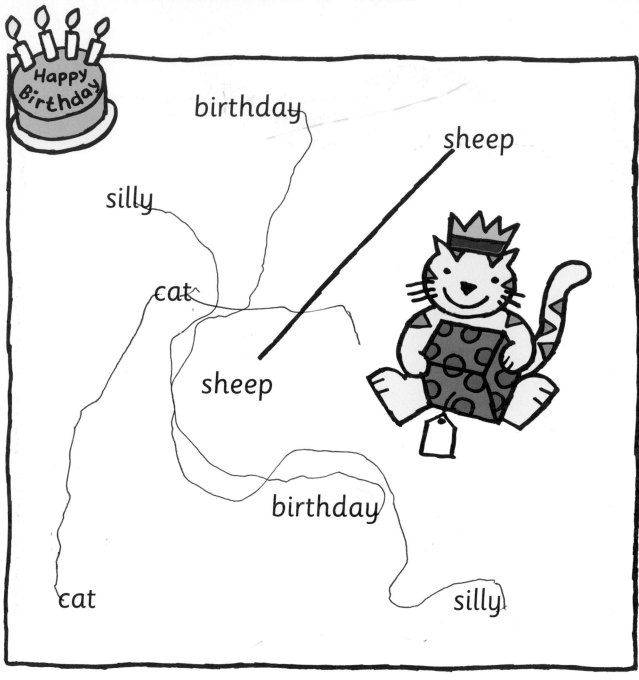

birthday

sheep

silly

cat

sheep

birthday

cat

silly

Do you know which word says 'cat'?
Draw a line from the word cat to the picture.
Try to remember what the word looks like, in case you see it again.

Clever you! Did you enjoy that?

Can you match these words?

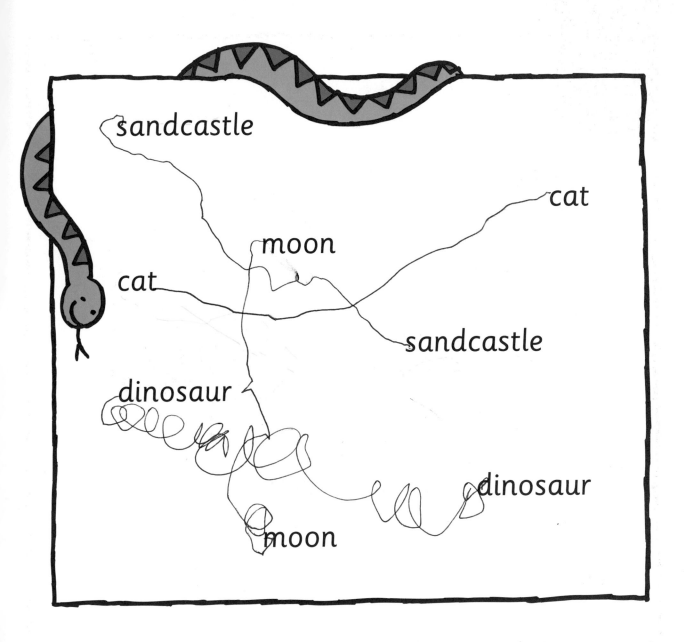

sandcastle

cat

moon

cat

sandcastle

dinosaur

dinosaur

moon

Can you see one that says 'cat' again? You may need to look back at the last page. If you remembered which one it was, that means you can read a word – cat. Put a circle round the cat word.

Note for parents: Look at the shape of the word 'cat' with your child. If s/he is ready, talk about the sounds and letters.

How about some more?

holly

Christmas

tree

present

tree

Christmas

snowman

holly

present

snowman

Note for parents: Choose a picture book in which a particular word appears often, ask your child to point to each example of the word.

Can you match these ones, too?

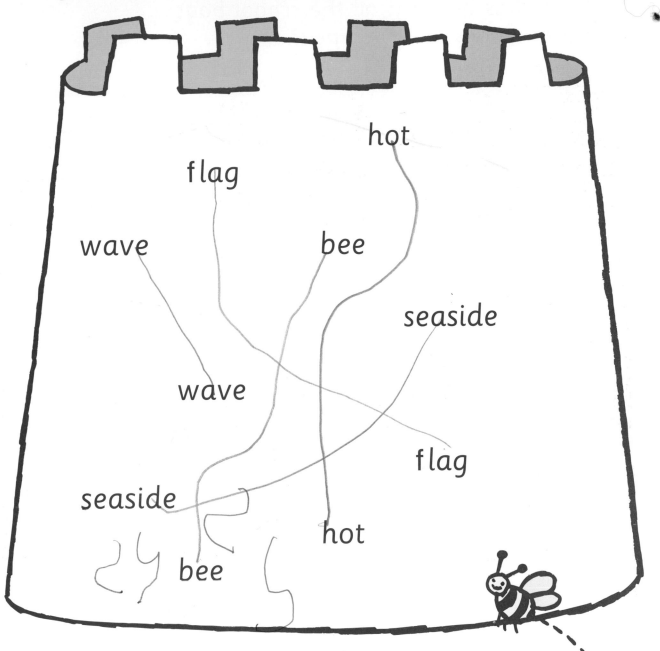

hot

flag

wave

bee

seaside

wave

flag

seaside

hot

bee

Which word says 'bee'?
Draw a line from the bee to the word.

Do you know what sound bee starts with?
Make the sound.

Can you help me?
Someone has dropped all the school bags.
Which one goes on which peg?

Thank you very much.

I think you deserve another sticker!

I need your help again.
Can you match each parcel to the right stocking?

You are so clever now.
Let's do some more difficult ones.
Look very closely.

book

sand

love

sand

book

love

Well done! Now try these.

jelly

sheep

giant

sheep

giant

jelly

 Note for parents: These are slightly harder because they are the same length, so your child needs to look more closely at the shapes within the words.

Let's practise some more like that.
Look very carefully.

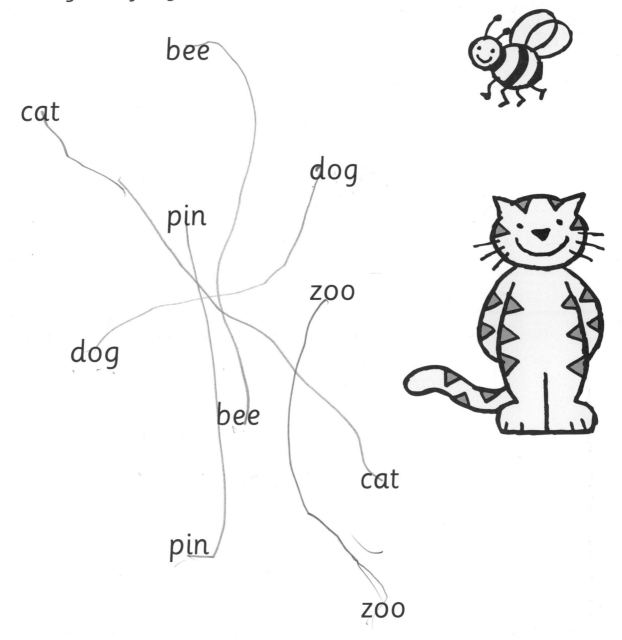

bee

cat

dog

pin

zoo

dog

bee

cat

pin

zoo

Can you remember which words say 'cat' and 'bee'?
Join a line from the words cat and bee
to the right pictures.

Now you are ready for these clever ones.
Look very carefully.

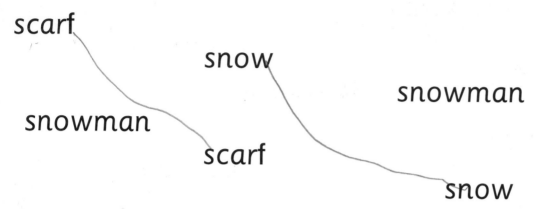

scarf

snow

snowman

snowman

scarf

snow

Was that easy?
Now try these.

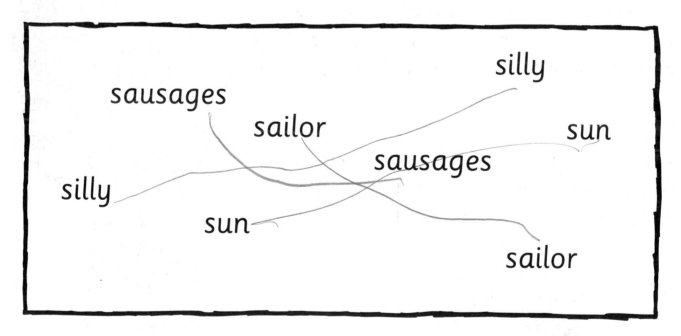

sausages

silly

sailor

sun

sausages

silly

sun

sailor

Easy peasy!

Note for parents: These words are harder because the child needs to look at more than just the first letter. This is an essential pre-reading skill.

Let's do some more.

sunny

tree

sausages

snowman

bee

Can you see a picture of a bee and a tree?
What sound does bee start with? b b b
What sound does tree start with? t t t

Look at the words again. Point to the first letters.
Which word do you think says 'bee'? Circle it in blue.
Which word do you think says 'tree'? Circle it in green.

Let's practise some more like that.

butterfly

bird

boy

bee

bags

What sound do the words start with?
Can you remember which one says 'bee'?
Which is the biggest word?
It says 'butterfly'.
Now listen to how the other words sound.
Which sounds the longest?
The one that sounds biggest looks biggest too.

Note for parents: This shows the sort of things you can talk about when looking at and listening to words.

You are clever enough to do this now.
Look at the word on the left.
Then find one the same along the same line.

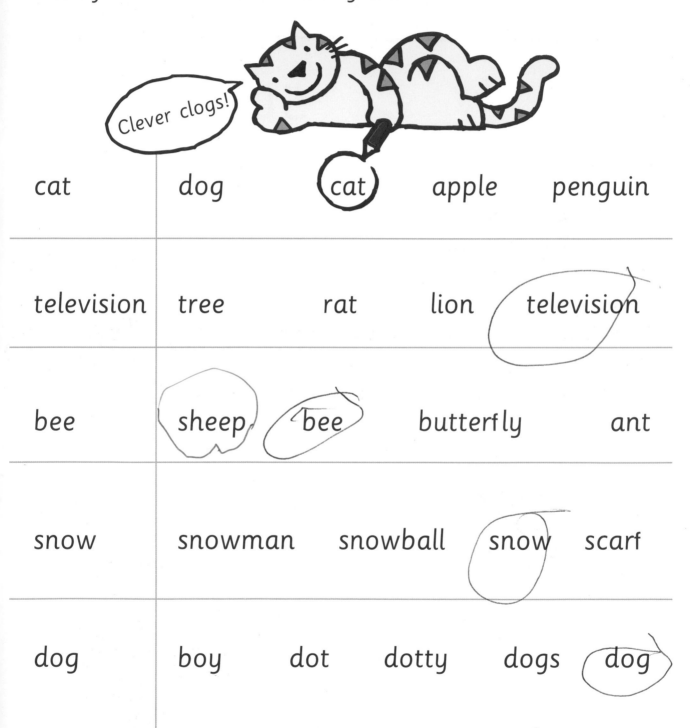

Clever clogs!

cat	dog	cat	apple	penguin
television	tree	rat	lion	television
bee	sheep	bee	butterfly	ant
snow	snowman	snowball	snow	scarf
dog	boy	dot	dotty	dogs	dog

You are learning such a lot. Clever you!

Sometimes writing is big and sometimes it is small.
If a word has exactly the same letters it is still the same
word. Can you match each small one to its bigger friend?

cat

happy

sun

boot

bee

sun

boot

cat

bee

happy

Note for parents: This is a new skill. Until now, your child
has had to match things which are exactly the same. Now
s/he starts to learn that some differences do not matter.

Can you do the same here?

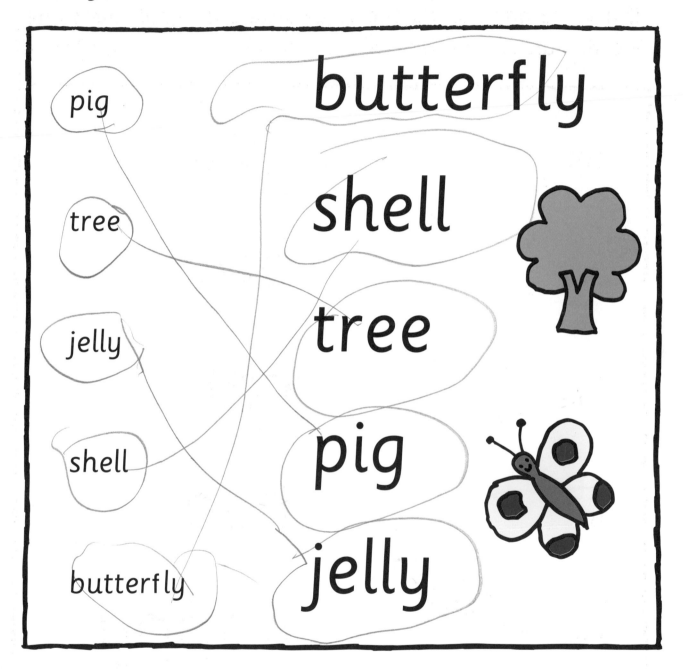

Ring in blue the words you think say 'butterfly'
(look for the first letter).
Ring in green the ones which say 'tree'.

Circle the first letter of each word.
Can you guess which word goes with which picture?
Join them with a line.

bee

tree

house

cat

Wonderful!

Let's do that again.

flag

tiger

mouse

apple

cake

lamp

Let's learn two words today.

Look at these little words:　　yes　　　no

Point to the first letter of yes and say the sound.
How many letters in yes?
Do the same for no.
Listen to the questions below.
You circle the right answer.

Great reader.

Do you like chocolate cake? 　yes　no

Do you like spiders on toast? 　yes　no

Can you fly? 　yes　no

Can you touch your nose? 　yes　no

Can you tickle the moon? 　yes　no

Do you have three legs? 　yes　no

Are you clever?　　yes　no

 You certainly are clever!

Let's read two more words.

big   small

Here are some big and small pictures. Join the big ones to the word that says '**big**' and the small ones to the word that says '**small**'.

Here is a picture of my house.
I have put some words on the picture.
Find the same words underneath and join them with
a line.

chimney

roof

window

door

garage

roof   chimney   window   garage   door

Can you draw curtains in my windows?
And colour the house? I'd like a **red** front door, please.

 You've really brightened up my house!

Here is a story about me going on a journey.
If you follow my paths with your finger you will
see what happens.

  Curly Cat packed his suitcase.

 He went to catch a train.

At night he arrived at the city.

 A man AND a dog chased him.

 Next day Curly Cat went home.

He was much happier!

Did you like that story?
I did not like the dog chasing me!

Note for parents: This teaches direction of print and story
sequence. When reading stories to your child, follow the print
with your finger from left to right.

Here is another story.
Can you do the same?

 On Monday I ate some fish.

 On Tuesday I ate some cake.

 On Wednesday I ate some cheese.

 On Thursday I drank some juice.

 On Friday I ate a pie.

 On Saturday I ate an apple.

 On Sunday I ate some ice cream.

Now you can make a story.
Look at the picture of my friend, Silly Cat.
He is wearing a silly hat.

Silly **cat** is wearing a silly **hat**.

A .... with a

silly ....

Well done!

Here is a word you know:

cat

Can you remember what it says?

I have written cat again a few times. But one of them is wrong. Circle the one that does not say cat.

cat   cat   cat   tac   cat   cat

What is wrong with it?
Yes, it's backwards, isn't it?

Try looking at this word now:

tree

Which one of these is the wrong way round?

tree   eert   tree   tree

Note for parents: Choose any word (perhaps your child's name to start with). Write it and cut it into separate letters, then ask your child to put the letters in order again.

Are you good at remembering things you see?
Choose a picture and look closely at the word below it.
Try to remember the word.

cat   tree   pig   lion

Cover the picture and its word.
Look at the words below and point to the word you remember.

tree	cat	lion	pig

Did you choose the right word? Check to see.
Now do the same with each of the other pictures.

Do you like stories?
You can make your own book. Here's how.

Note for parents: Making books with your child helps all the skills covered so far. It is practical, inter-active, and enjoyable for your child.

Start by making the blank pages, sticking them together and making the cover. You should have one short sentence and a picture on every page. Give lots of help but make sure your child feels that it is her/his book.

Here are some ideas for different books:

1. A book about your child. 'I am Sam. I am 4. I have a sister called Sarah. Here is my house. Here is my dog, Barney. Here is my mum.'

2. A diary. 'On Monday I went to the beach. On Tuesday I played with Jack ...'

3. A rhyming words book. 'Here is a man. The man has a van. The man ran to the van. He was hot so he needed a fan ...'

Perhaps you could read to your teddies – they would like that.

Note for parents: Carry on reading lots of stories to your child. Story time should be relaxed, cosy and happy. This will help your child to enjoy reading later.